PHL

KT-465-363
54060000059542

C

A MEDIEVAL CASTLE

Series Editor	David Salariya
Book Editor	Shirley Willis
Design Assistant	Carol Attwood
Consultant	John Gillingham

Author:

Fiona Macdonald studied history at Cambridge University and at the University of East Anglia. She has taught children, adults and undergraduates. She has written many books on historical topics, mainly for children.

Illustrator:

Mark Bergin was born in Hastings in 1961. He studied at Eastbourne College of Art and has specialized in historical reconstruction since leaving art school in 1983.

Consultant:

John Gillingham studied history at Oxford and Munich universities. Since 1966 he has taught history at the London School of Economics and Political Science. He is the author of books on Richard the Lionheart, the Angevine Empire and The Wars of the Roses. He has also written and presented a T.V. programme on the Magna Carta.

First published in 1990 by
Simon and Schuster Young Books

Published in paperback in 1996, 1997 and 1999 by
Macdonald Young Books
an imprint of Wayland Publishers Limited
61 Western Road
Hove
East Sussex
BN3 1JD

941MAC

THE BRITISH MUSEUM WITHDRAWN
THE PAUL HAMLYN LIBRARY

You can find Macdonald Young Books on the internet at
http://www.wayland.co.uk

© The Salariya Book Co Ltd 1990

All rights reserved. No part of this book may be reproduced, stored in a retrieval system, or transmitted in any form or by any means, electronic, mechanical, photocopying, recording or otherwise, without the prior permission of the copyright owner.

British Library Cataloguing in Publication Data
Macdonald, Fiona
  A medieval castle. – (Inside story)
  1. Great Britain. Castles, history
  1. Title 11. Series
  941

ISBN 0-7500-2352-X (PB)

Typeset by Central Southern Typesetters (Hove) Ltd

Printed in Portugal by Edições ASA

INSIDE STORY

A MEDIEVAL CASTLE

FIONA MACDONALD   MARK BERGIN

MACDONALD YOUNG BOOKS

CONTENTS

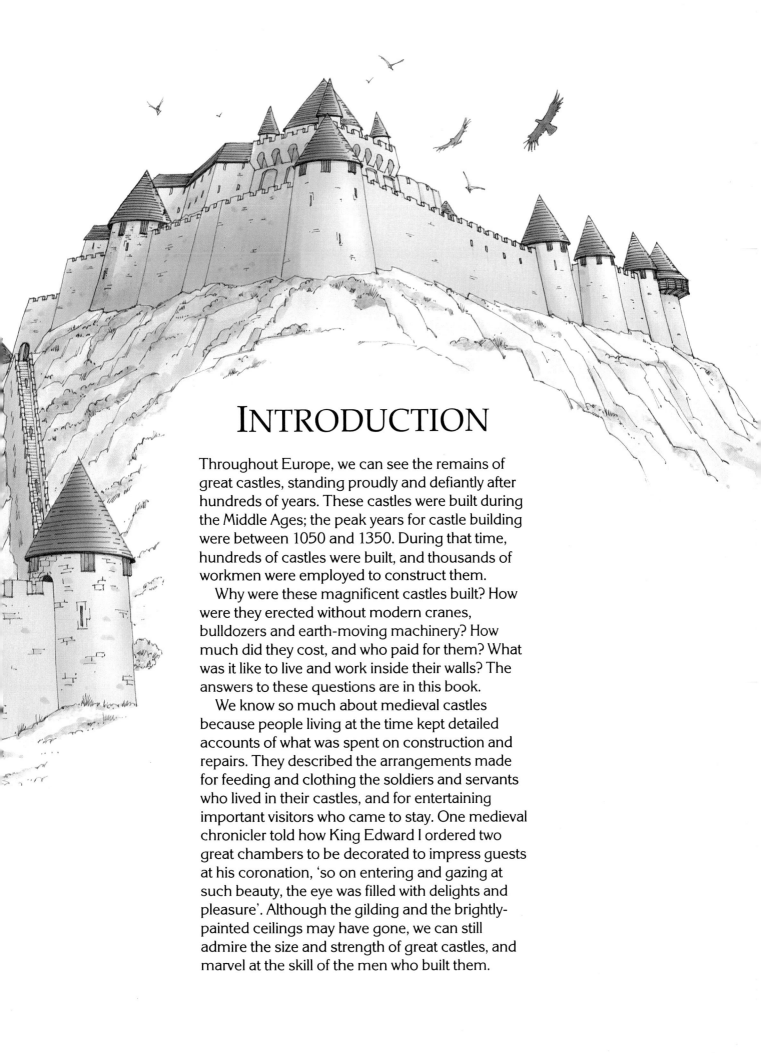

INTRODUCTION

Throughout Europe, we can see the remains of great castles, standing proudly and defiantly after hundreds of years. These castles were built during the Middle Ages; the peak years for castle building were between 1050 and 1350. During that time, hundreds of castles were built, and thousands of workmen were employed to construct them.

Why were these magnificent castles built? How were they erected without modern cranes, bulldozers and earth-moving machinery? How much did they cost, and who paid for them? What was it like to live and work inside their walls? The answers to these questions are in this book.

We know so much about medieval castles because people living at the time kept detailed accounts of what was spent on construction and repairs. They described the arrangements made for feeding and clothing the soldiers and servants who lived in their castles, and for entertaining important visitors who came to stay. One medieval chronicler told how King Edward I ordered two great chambers to be decorated to impress guests at his coronation, 'so on entering and gazing at such beauty, the eye was filled with delights and pleasure'. Although the gilding and the brightly-painted ceilings may have gone, we can still admire the size and strength of great castles, and marvel at the skill of the men who built them.

CHOOSING THE SITE

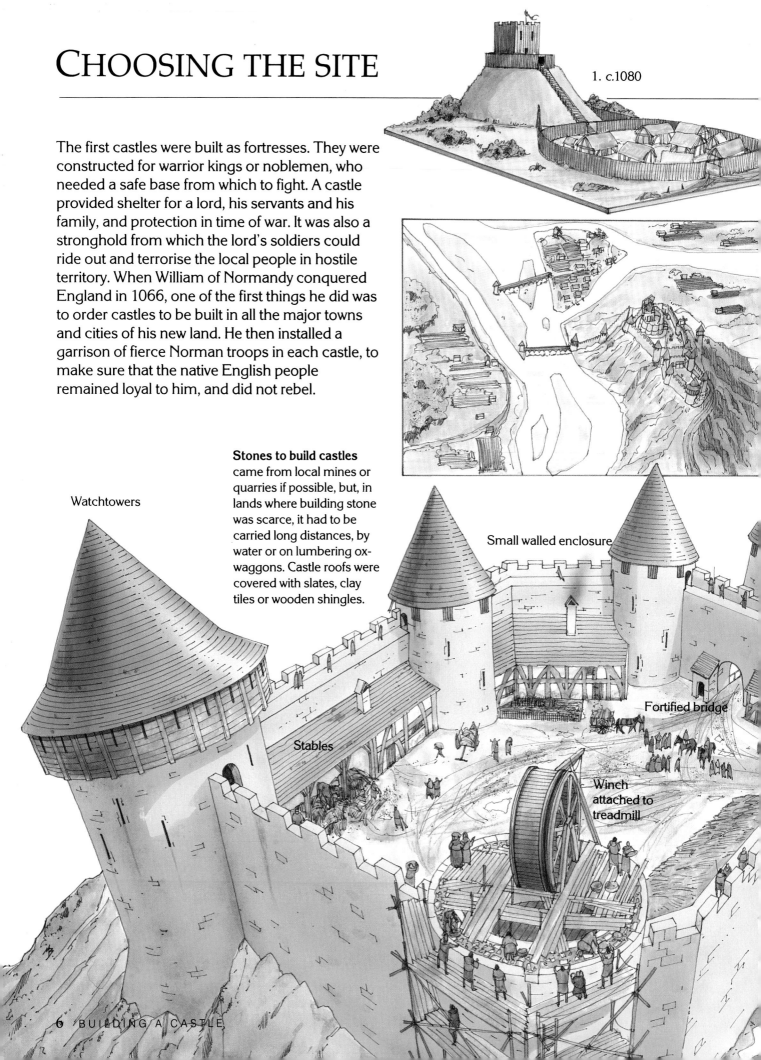

1. c.1080

The first castles were built as fortresses. They were constructed for warrior kings or noblemen, who needed a safe base from which to fight. A castle provided shelter for a lord, his servants and his family, and protection in time of war. It was also a stronghold from which the lord's soldiers could ride out and terrorise the local people in hostile territory. When William of Normandy conquered England in 1066, one of the first things he did was to order castles to be built in all the major towns and cities of his new land. He then installed a garrison of fierce Norman troops in each castle, to make sure that the native English people remained loyal to him, and did not rebel.

Stones to build castles came from local mines or quarries if possible, but, in lands where building stone was scarce, it had to be carried long distances, by water or on lumbering ox-waggons. Castle roofs were covered with slates, clay tiles or wooden shingles.

Watchtowers

Small walled enclosure

Stables

Fortified bridge

Winch attached to treadmill

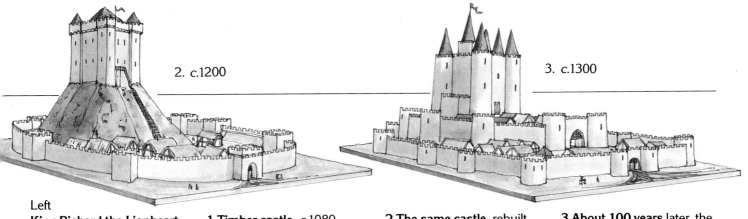

2. c.1200

3. c.1300

Left
King Richard the Lionheart chose a strongly defended site, on a cliff above the River Seine, in France, to build his favourite castle, Château Gaillard. The river forms a barrier on one side, while rocky slopes make it difficult to attack from the other sides. The castle is surrounded by a strong 'curtain' wall. A new village grew up nearby to house all the construction workers.

1 Timber castle, c.1080. The tower is built on an artificial mound (or motte); the outbuildings are surrounded by a strong fence. (The outer enclosure is called a bailey.)

2 The same castle, rebuilt c.1200. The timber tower has been replaced by a strong stone keep, with fortifications at each corner. The fence around the bailey is replaced by a stone wall.

3 About 100 years later, the stone castle has been enlarged and strengthened still further. There are new, rounded towers (built in the latest fashion) and an extra defending wall.

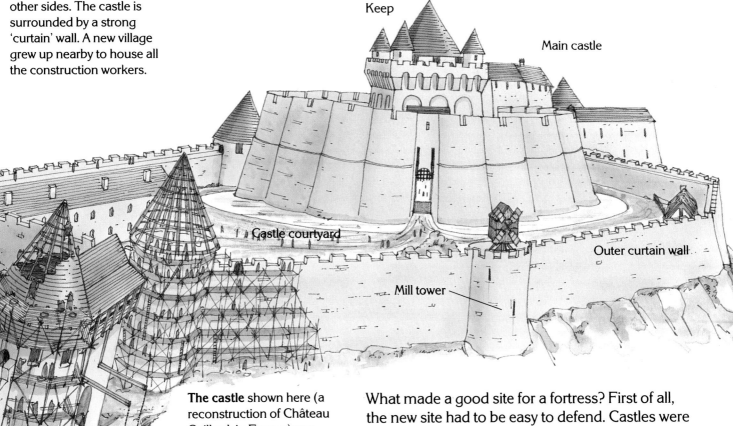

Keep

Main castle

Castle courtyard

Mill tower

Outer curtain wall

Drawbridge

Moat

The castle shown here (a reconstruction of Château Gaillard, in France) was designed by the best military architects of the 12th century. The main castle courtyard is linked to a smaller walled enclosure by a fortified bridge. There is a strong central tower with a massive inner defensive wall, surrounded by an outer 'curtain' wall, with watchtowers.

What made a good site for a fortress? First of all, the new site had to be easy to defend. Castles were built on steep hillsides or at the top of rocky cliffs. On flat land, where there were no hills, artificial mounds of rocks and earth were created instead. Other castles were built along the coast, on islands or on river-promontories. Because castles had to control the surrounding countryside, they might be built astride mountain passes, or at river-crossings, or at the junctions of major roads. In that way, no one – whether friend or enemy – could pass by without the castle guards' permission.

BUILDING THE CASTLE

The earliest castles were built of earth and wood. Local timber was used if possible, for economy and convenience. A vast amount of wood was needed to build a big castle: over 8,000 oaks (about 800,000 square metres of forest) were felled to construct the huge fortress of Trelleborg in Sweden.

By the 12th century, most new castles were being built in stone, which made them better able to withstand attack. Unlike wood, stone could not be set on fire; and, unlike the earlier wooden fences and towers, stone walls could be built several metres thick. It was almost impossible for enemy forces to batter holes in them, until gunpowder was brought to Europe from China in the 14th century. These new castles were designed with more space for the lord and his family, and with better quarters for the servants and soldiers.

A castle under siege had to be able to provide for all its inhabitants for many months; capacious storerooms for food, fuel and weapons were therefore essential. They occupied the ground floor of the castle keep. The upper floors, where people lived and worked, could not usually be reached from the courtyard. Instead, a ladder gave access to the upper rooms, but could be hauled inside if an enemy approached. In some castles the staircase was in a separate building, linked to the main rooms by a drawbridge.

Winch and treadmill

Dungeon

Below
In winter, workmen took shelter in wooden huts, called lodges. They continued to work on details of the castle building – doorways, windows or decorative carvings – even when it was too wet or frosty to work outside.

Right
Castle walls usually had three layers: a rough stone inner shell, a thick, solid filling of flint and rubble, and a strong outer casing of stone, called ashlar. In the great hall, stonework might be decoratively carved.

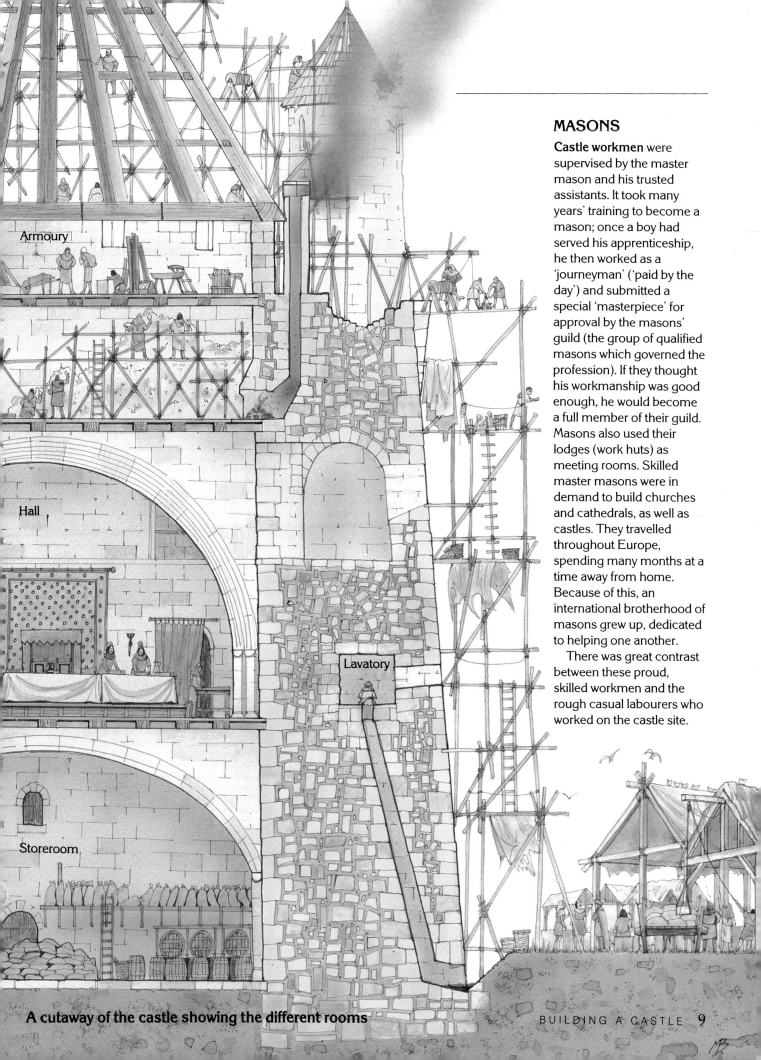

Armoury

Hall

Storeroom

Lavatory

MASONS

Castle workmen were supervised by the master mason and his trusted assistants. It took many years' training to become a mason; once a boy had served his apprenticeship, he then worked as a 'journeyman' ('paid by the day') and submitted a special 'masterpiece' for approval by the masons' guild (the group of qualified masons which governed the profession). If they thought his workmanship was good enough, he would become a full member of their guild. Masons also used their lodges (work huts) as meeting rooms. Skilled master masons were in demand to build churches and cathedrals, as well as castles. They travelled throughout Europe, spending many months at a time away from home. Because of this, an international brotherhood of masons grew up, dedicated to helping one another.

There was great contrast between these proud, skilled workmen and the rough casual labourers who worked on the castle site.

A cutaway of the castle showing the different rooms

CRAFTSMEN AND BUILDERS

Wood was sometimes toughened by leaving it to soak in water all winter. This made sawing very hard work.

The men who built the medieval castles worked extremely hard. They had some machinery to help them – pulleys, winches, and other lifting gear – but the difficult work of construction was done by hand. Stone was cut to size and lifted into position using hand-powered tools. The huge timbers used for scaffolding and to construct the castles floors and rafters were sawed and shaped by hand. Some castle inhabitants lived in the middle of a building site for years; it might easily take a lifetime to rebuild a great castle in the latest style.

In emergencies, however, castles could be erected with amazing speed. King Edward I's eight new castles, built under wartime conditions as English strongholds against the Welsh, were ready to occupy in under ten years. By 1296, the king was employing over 2,630 workmen in a hurried attempt to finish Conwy castle, at a cost of over £250 a week. (By comparison, a knight might have an income of one or two pounds a week.)

Skilled workmen were organised into teams led by a master mason (or master carpenter or master plumber, if they worked in wood or lead). They were helped by gangs of unskilled labourers, and by local workers and apprentices. Often, the labourers were unwilling 'volunteers': soldiers drafted in to help, out-of-work farmhands, and prisoners, released on parole.

A DAY IN THE LIFE OF A WORKMAN

5.30 am Sunrise. Breakfast (bread, cheese, weak cider). Leaves house to walk to work.

7 am Meets up with other workers, including forced labourers, who live in camp on the site.

7.15 am Discusses the progress of the section he's working on with the foreman of his team, a master mason.

7.30 am Workmen fill in outer walls with rubble. Mason starts carving arched window frame.

8.30 am Advises a young apprentice who has recently started to work with his master.

9 am Surprise arrival of a load of stone. Delivery is late because the waggons got stuck in the mud.

10 am The main meal of the day. The workmen eat bread, pork and lentil stew, and drink ale or cider.

10.45 am Back to the masons' yard. It is summer-time, and hammering the stone is hot and tiring work.

1 pm A workman nearby falls off the scaffolding. A servant rushes off on horseback to find a doctor.

Scaffolding was made from wooden poles, tied together with strong rope. Wheels and pulleys were also made of timber.

4 pm The day's work is nearly over. The master mason comes to check on the carving.

6 pm Back home, to a welcome supper of soup and cheese. Time to relax, then to bed about 10 pm.

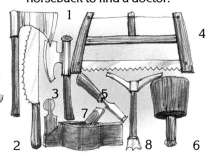

Carpenters' tools: 1. axe 2. saw 3. anvil hammer 4. frame saw 5. chisel 6. mallet 7. plane 8. auger.

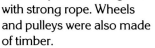

CASTLE DESIGN

The earliest castle buildings were designed to provide the headquarters for a local lord and his knights, and shelter for occupying armies or for terrified local people facing an attack, but they were not pleasant or convenient places in which to live. Extra buildings soon grew up on many castle sites, to cater for the needs of all who worked there, or for those, who, like the lord and his lady, came to stay at the castle from time to time.

There might be a brewhouse, a laundry, a huge baker's oven to supply fresh bread, workshops, dovecotes and stables.

Later castles were surrounded by larger, but still strongly defended, open spaces. New stone-built walls were constructed to encircle gardens, orchards, fishponds, and exercise yards, where horses could be ridden and soldiers could practise wrestling or archery. Towers were built at intervals along these walls, to strengthen them, and also to provide extra accommodation for castle workers or visitors.

Inside the castle, living conditions became more comfortable. Rich tapestries hung on the stone walls of the great hall, and stopped some, but not all, of the draughts. Separate chambers were built for the lord and his family, where they could sit quietly, away from the noise and bustle of the hall. And, after about 1200, primitive lavatories (holes in the wall) began to be installed. Castle life was becoming more civilised.

Great chamber

Steward's tower

Great ha

Storeroom

Chapel

The defensive walls surrounding a castle were often several metres thick, and composed of a double skin of masonry, with a space in between. This was used to provide living quarters for servants, or for visitors. There was usually a walkway running along the top of the walls, from which the castle guards could keep watch. The walls were topped with battlements ('shields' of stone with gaps between them), which allowed defenders to fire down on an enemy while remaining under cover.

Most castles were designed to include a whole range of facilities, such as a well to ensure the supply of drinking water, a windmill to grind corn into flour, and a chapel for prayers.

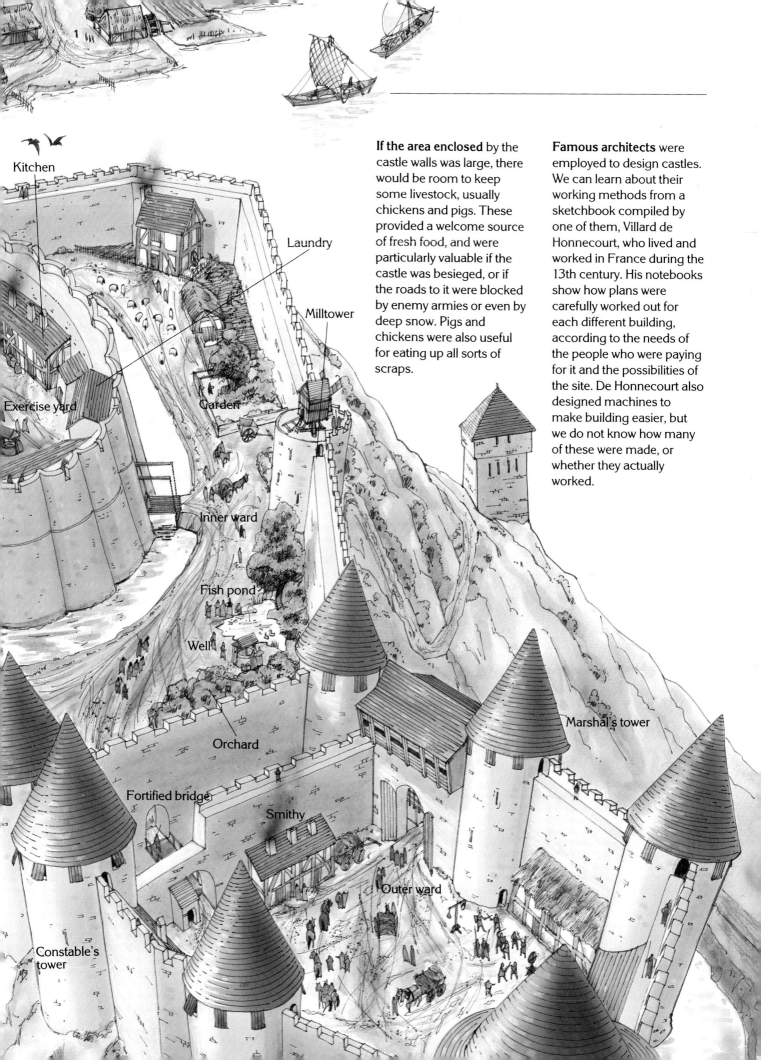

Kitchen

Laundry

Milltower

Exercise yard

Garden

Inner ward

Fish pond

Well

Orchard

Marshal's tower

Fortified bridge

Smithy

Outer ward

Constable's tower

If the area enclosed by the castle walls was large, there would be room to keep some livestock, usually chickens and pigs. These provided a welcome source of fresh food, and were particularly valuable if the castle was besieged, or if the roads to it were blocked by enemy armies or even by deep snow. Pigs and chickens were also useful for eating up all sorts of scraps.

Famous architects were employed to design castles. We can learn about their working methods from a sketchbook compiled by one of them, Villard de Honnecourt, who lived and worked in France during the 13th century. His notebooks show how plans were carefully worked out for each different building, according to the needs of the people who were paying for it and the possibilities of the site. De Honnecourt also designed machines to make building easier, but we do not know how many of these were made, or whether they actually worked.

THE WORLD OF THE CASTLE

Lord   Lady   Reeve   Clerk   Priest   Marshal

The lord and lady were married when they were young – it was usually arranged by their parents, who sought rich or noble partners.

Every lord wanted an heir, to inherit his estates. But perhaps half the children born in the Middle Ages died before they were 15 years old.

The lord and lady also had a staff of clerks, who knew how to read, write and keep accounts. When they were away from their castles, lords sent instructions on by letter.

The lord kept a staff to help him run his estates. The steward was in charge of the castle household; reeves and bailiffs organised the lord's farms and collected rents.

Steward   Taster   Pantler   Butler   Ewerer   Chief cook

Lodgings for the castle household were organised by the marshal. He had grooms, pages and serving maids to help him. They made sure the rooms were ready for visitors.

In royal castles, there might also be a taster, to sample the food prepared for the royal family, and make sure that it was not poisoned. As you might expect, his was a well-paid job.

The butler and pantler were responsible for buying and storing supplies of food and drink for the castle household. The ewerer provided clean cloths to cover the lord's table.

Cooks worked in the hot, steamy kitchen. Normally, kitchens were built in the castle courtyard, to lessen the risk of fire. Medieval people liked two hot meals a day, and strong, spicy food.

A castle was not only a fortress. It was also a family home, an army barracks and a business head-quarters, where the lord's officials collected rents, administered his estates and enforced law and order. A great castle was rather like a small town. Inside its walls, you could find almost everything you needed, from medicinal herbs to a blacksmith skilled at mending armour, and maybe even a musician or fortune-teller, crouched in some dim corner of the great hall, ready to amuse you.

A wealthy lord might own several castles, and smaller farms and manor houses as well. He would usually spend only a few weeks each year at any one of them. But castles did not stand empty while

Archer   Crossbowman   Knights   Juggler   Jesters   Musicians

The castle's defences were very important. Lords kept a staff of loyal followers even during peacetime. Occasionally, fighting broke out between the followers of rival lords.

The castle would usually be guarded by a number of foot-soldiers: men who fought with longbows and crossbows, or pikes and staves.

Jugglers, acrobats, jesters and minstrels all came to the castle to entertain. Favourite instruments among travelling minstrels included lutes and bagpipes.

A feast would sometimes end with music and dancing; lords and ladies danced with their guests, while the servants danced with each other.

Carver   Cupbearer   Mat weavers   Falconer   Spinner   Groom   Sweeper

Carving meat, pouring wine and offering food to guests was an elaborate art. Diners were served in order of rank: kings, lords and ladies first, ordinary people later. The servants ate simple food.

Castle floors were covered with a layer of straw or rushes, which could be swept away and replaced when they became dirty. Later, rushes were woven into thick mats.

Ordinary people's clothes were made of coarse wool or linen, spun and woven by hand. Lords and ladies slept between fine linen sheets, which were laundered and repaired in the castle.

Grooms looked after the lord and lady's favourite horses, as well as the heavier horses ridden to war. Sweepers were employed to keep the courtyards clean.

the lord was absent. Maintaining the castle provided full-time work for a number of people.

As well as essential building repairs, wood had to be gathered for cooking and heating, rushes had to be cut for floor-coverings and all kinds of foodstuffs had to be salted and preserved for the winter or in case of a siege. All year round, there were horses and poultry to be fed and cared for; and in summer, fresh flowers and vegetables were grown in the kitchen garden, or in tubs and boxes ranged along the battlements. Every week, tapestries and bedcovers had to be shaken free of dust, lice and fleas. But the worst task, surely, was cleaning out the smelly lavatories, ditches and moats.

FOOD AND DRINK

Grapes were pressed to make wine, which was often drunk hot, with spices. Poor people drank cider, weak ale or water. Honey or liquorice was sometimes used to disguise the taste of stale or tainted water.

A castle had to be well-stocked with food at all times. There was a large garrison of hungry soldiers to feed, and even in peaceful years, the cooks and scullions might suddenly have to cater for a party of perhaps fifty hungry and unexpected guests, although it was more usual for the lord or lady to warn the castle steward of such a visit.

It was even more important for a castle to be well-provisioned in time of war. Enemy soldiers would surround the castle, cutting off contact with the outside world. They would destroy all crops and foodstuffs they could find in the locality. When this happened, a well-stocked larder could literally mean the difference between life and death for the inhabitants of the castle.

Food was preserved in a number of different ways. Meat and fish were salted, smoked or dried; fruit and vegetables were pickled; grapes were made into wine or verjuice (rather like vinegar, and useful as a preservative); milk was turned into salted butter and hard, long-lasting cheese. Apples and pears were preserved in cool attics, and honey was carefully stored in sealed jars. Mushrooms were gathered from the fields and threaded on long strings to dry. Pungent vegetables like onions and garlic, precious spices and dried herbs were used to disguise the taste of stale preserved meat, and savoury dishes were often flavoured with fruit or honey as well.

Meat for the winter was salted in huge wooden vats. Large quantities of salt were purchased each year for use by the castle's cooks. Salt was expensive; it was made by evaporating sea water in shallow lagoons.

Salting meat

One noble household ate the following food on 24th June 1319: Half a carcase of salt beef, a small side of bacon, half a pig, and some mutton. Forty herrings, 2 salt cod, 2 ling, half a salmon, some whiting and some eels. Two ducks, 6 hens, 13 pullets, 150 eggs and a pennyworth of milk. Large amounts of bread were bought, also 40 gallons (about 150 litres) of ale and 8 gallons (45 litres) of wine.

At least 50 people were fed, probably for three meals, and the total cost was just over £1 (perhaps about £300 today).

Herbs used in cooking

1. Spoons and knives
2. Roast peacocks were eaten at special meals.
3. Sweet violet
4. Parsley
5. Primrose
6. Borage
7. Pot hanger
8. Meat hook
9. Decorated pie
10. Decorated roast pheasant

This brass monument commemorates Guillaume Tirel, cook to King Philip VI of France. He was so good at his job that he was granted a coat of arms by the king.

Candles were made from beeswax; those for every-day use were made from animal fat, chiefly tallow from sheep. Wicks were made from thread or rushes.

Labour-saving devices were not available to help with cooking; food was chopped or pounded by hand. Recipes included pies baked in pastry 'coffyns'.

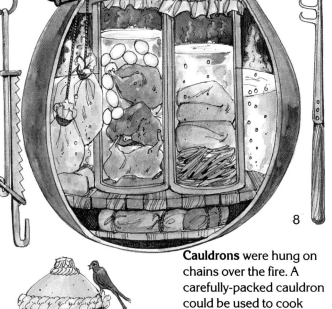

Cauldrons were hung on chains over the fire. A carefully-packed cauldron could be used to cook different items at once: here, stew with onions, boiled fish, and oatmeal puddings.

Flour for the castle was ground at the lord's windmill. The miller produced different grades: fine, to make white bread for the lord, or coarse, to make brown bread for the servants.

Bread was baked in brick ovens, heated by burning wood inside them, and then raking out the ashes. Loaves were laid on the hot oven floor using wooden shovels, or 'peels'.

MEALS AND MANNERS

Medieval cooks were skilled at preparing elaborate food for special occasions, or to honour important guests. When the lord was in residence, meals were served with great ceremony. The main meal of the day was eaten at about 10 am, and it could last for two or three hours. It would consist of several courses, each with a variety of different dishes. The diners would help themselves to what they wanted to eat – using their fingers, or the point of a knife; forks were not yet in common use. It was good manners to select a particularly succulent morsel from the serving dish and offer it to your neighbour. Cups and plates might also be shared; men with moustaches were warned not to leave a film of grease floating on the wine after they had drunk, as it would offend the ladies.

The lord, his family and their guests sat apart from the rest of the household, at a 'high table', raised above the level of the rest of the hall. They were served first. Kings and princes employed men to taste their food before they ate it, to make sure that it was not poisoned. Food was carved

Before starting to eat, the lord and his guests would wash their hands. Then one of the castle priests would say grace.

Medieval lords and ladies ate a great deal of meat. They were especially fond of game (venison, pheasant, partridge and hare) cooked in thick, spicy sauces. The Church taught that people ought to eat fish instead of meat on Wednesdays and Fridays, but many people chose to ignore this rule and pay a fine instead.

Ordinary people ate more vegetables, mostly cooked in soups or stews. (Raw fruit and vegetables were believed to be unhealthy.) Cabbages, leeks and garlic were popular, also a thick porridge made from dried peas or beans. A kilo of bread per day was the minimum for people who worked hard on the land. There were no potatoes, and rice was a luxury. A noble feast might end with a 'subtlety' made out of pastry, sugar and marzipan.

and brought to table by young boys from noble families who had been sent to the castle to learn good manners, polished speech, and all the rules of upper-class behaviour. Soldiers and servants had plainer food; leftovers were fed to the pigs, or offered to the poor.

A busy medieval kitchen

Meals were served on trenchers, thick slices of coarse brown bread which were used as plates, or to fit inside costly silver dishes. They soaked up grease and sauces from the food. If you were very hungry, you could break small pieces off your trencher and eat it; at the end of the meal, trenchers were gathered up and given to the beggars who gathered outside the castle gate. There were always dogs, sniffing round the diners in the hall in search of titbits, though it was not considered good manners to feed them from the table.

CASTLE AND COMMUNITY

A castle was usually the largest building for miles around. Often it stood in wild and lonely countryside, but even when it was built on the edge of a town its walls towered over everything else, except, perhaps, the spires of a newly-finished cathedral. Its looming presence meant safety and security for everyone who lived nearby.

For this reason, many villages and towns grew up under the protection of great castles. Such new settlements were usually encouraged by the lord; the villagers, men and women, provided a labour force to work in his fields, while their sons and daughters were useful as servants in the castle.

In return for permission to settle on the lord's land, the villagers had to work part of the time for him, and also give him a share of their crops, or else a yearly money rent. He insisted that they used his mill to grind all their corn into flour (and he charged them for doing it), and he collected tolls on all goods sold in the village market place. Sometimes, villagers even contributed to the cost of keeping the castle walls in good repair.

In spite of these charges, which poor villagers could ill-afford, castle settlements grew and prospered. If a marauding army was on the rampage, the presence of a strong castle nearby was one of the best guarantees of a village's safety. In this way, castles helped to prevent war, too.

The village houses were surrounded by cultivated fields. There were owned by the lord, but mostly farmed by the villagers in return for work on the lord's own land, or for an annual money payment. There was also rough grazing land for sheep and cattle, and meadows for hay. The village illustrated here is on the banks of a wide river; it has a quay where boats can tie up, and a customs house where the lord's officials collect tolls and taxes.

Most village houses had only one room, where the family worked, ate and slept. By the 14th century, separate first-floor rooms for sleeping were being added to the larger houses. Heating came from a smoky fire in the centre of the downstairs room; windows were closed with wooden shutters. The floor was made of beaten earth, and there was very little furniture – a mattress, a bench, some stools and a chest for storing valuables.

A typical village would have its own church, a mill driven by wind or water, a well for water and a village green, where children could play and where minor criminals were punished.

Village houses, except in areas where building stone was easy to find, were made of timber frames, filled in with wattle (woven twigs) and daub (clay mixed with straw or horsehair). Their roofs were usually thatched with reeds or wheat straw.

THE VILLAGE FAIR

Everyone looked forward to a fair. Once or twice a year, villagers from miles around – and also, unfortunately, all the local pickpockets and petty thieves – made their way to the open space outside the castle gates. There they found travelling merchants busily setting up their stalls, jostling the heavily-laden pedlars who staggered in from the countryside. Delicious smells wafted from the booths selling hot pies, spiced wine and gingerbread, almost overpowering the more sinister odours which could be traced to heaps of newly-tanned leather, leaky barrels of fish, and stacks of cheap tallow candles.

For most villagers, this was their only chance to buy goods from other places. Perhaps fine woollen cloth, woven in England or Flanders, or soft gloves and slippers made by skilful leatherworkers in Spain. Young men gazed longingly at elegantly decorated swords and daggers from Germany. Village women marvelled at the beautiful silks and brocades from Italy and China. Only the lord and lady in the castle could afford to buy them.

But it did not cost very much to enjoy all the entertainment that was on offer at the fair. Musicians, jugglers, acrobats and trained animals would perform for a penny, or even less. There was also the chance to catch up on local news and gossip, and to meet friends and relations.

Wealthy merchants travelled to fairs, where they set up their tents to receive visitors and strike bargains with local tradesmen.

THE FARMER'S YEAR

JANUARY
The New Year was a time for celebration, and for feasting with friends and neighbours.

FEBRUARY
Firewood was cut from dead trees. Wood was the main source of fuel.

MARCH
Pruning vines in early spring. Only the strongest shoots were left to fruit.

APRIL
Men and women weeding crops. If left, the weeds would choke the crops.

MAY
Inspecting beehives. Honey provided sweetness; sugar was a luxury.

JUNE
Hay had to be cut and dried in fine weather to provide animals' winter feed.

JULY
Harvesting corn. Everyone joined in the harvest; if it failed, they would go hungry.

AUGUST
Threshing with flails to separate the grains from the husks.

SEPTEMBER
Treading the grapes to make wine. Grapes were also sun-dried to make raisins.

OCTOBER
Sowing corn. The grains were scattered by hand over the fields.

NOVEMBER
Villagers had grazing rights on rough pasture and wasteland.

DECEMBER
Pigs were killed and their meat was preserved by salting or smoking.

FARMERS AND FARMING

Stores for the winter

Thatching was a skilled job, and very hard work. Over 10,000 bundles of reeds were needed to thatch a barn. Straw might also be used.

Repairing thatch

Weaving and spinning

Oak barrel with tap

Flaxbeater

The kings and lords who built the medieval castles were the richest men of their time. Their wealth came from the land; partly from the crops produced on their own farms and partly from rents and taxes paid by the peasants who lived on their estates.

Medieval farming was highly organised. By the 13th century, farm managers were beginning to write books, telling other farmers how best to tend their crops and animals. According to them, an ideal farm was self-sufficient; it produced everything needed to support the farmer and his family, with enough left over to sell for cash, so that he could pay rents and taxes to his lord, and wages to any workers he needed to hire.

Depending on the local soil and climate, the farmer might specialise in growing grain or rearing livestock. Wherever he lived, he would probably keep a couple of cows to provide fresh milk, butter and cream for his family, a few pigs, and maybe a goat or two. The farmer's wife would rear chickens, and sell eggs and plump young hens at the market to earn some pocket money. She would also be busy cooking and preserving food, caring for sick animals, looking after her children, and spinning thread for sale to travelling merchants, or to weave into rough cloth for her family to wear.

This farmer is fortunate. He has a well on his own land, and does not have to send servants down to the village each day to fetch clean drinking water.

Both men and women worked as labourers on the farm. Men did the ploughing, sowing and carting, while women weeded the crops and cared for animals.

Female servants helped the farmer's wife to cook, preserve food, brew ale and make butter and cheese. They might also gather herbs to make medicines.

Scythe

Well

Plough

Churn

A prosperous farmhouse in the early 15th century. The farmer cultivates about 100 acres of land, and employs between 10 and 20 labourers, depending on the season. His wife also has servants to help her. The farmer has a farmhouse, and a substantial barn. There are stables for his horses and cattle, cartsheds, and a covered yard for his sheep.

The farmer owns a cart, and at least two horse-drawn ploughs as well as scythes for cutting grass, forks and spades for lifting and digging, and sickles for reaping corn. His wife has a weaving loom and a well-equipped kitchen. She also has a churn for making butter, and a new oak barrel, with a tap, in which her home-brewed ale is stored.

LORDS AND LADIES

Life in the castle was organised to please the lord and lady. In peacetime country castles were used as hunting lodges, or as healthy retreats from dirty and disease-ridden towns. There was the chance to relax and greet visitors, or enjoy songs and poems newly-composed by favourite minstrels.

In whichever castle he was, the lord had to deal with bundles of documents needing his attention. Possibly an urgent summons to attend the king's court, or a petition from poor villagers explaining why they could not pay their taxes. He had to inspect the annual accounts drawn up by his steward and bailiff. He might receive letters from merchants trading overseas, or secret messages from conspirators seeking his support.

A great lord might be away, on government business or at war for months at a time. Often, he left his wife in charge of all his castles, trusting her to ensure that everything ran smoothly during his absence. Noblewomen were taught from childhood how to manage a large household, how to give orders to servants, and how to keep accounts. Occasionally, they even had to organise the defence of a castle when it was attacked. One 14th-century lady, Joan of Flanders, fought off her husband's enemies, and was described as having 'the courage of a man and the heart of a lion'.

On special occasions, lords and ladies wore magnificent clothes, made of brilliantly-dyed wool or rich silk and velvet, lavishly embroidered and trimmed with fur. Men as well as women wore jewellery, and both sexes perfumed their hair and their gloves. Nobles' clothes were extremely expensive, and were expected to last a lifetime. Sometimes they were bequeathed to relatives or friends in wills. Both lords and ladies followed fashion, with fantastic hats and narrow, pointed shoes. Clergymen preached against such extravagances. The Church taught that rich people had a duty to give to the poor, but there was a great contrast between the rich man in his castle and the beggars huddled outside.

Below left
Washing and taking baths were popular; sometimes the lord and lady bathed together.

Lords, and sometimes ladies, administered justice on behalf of the king. Criminals might be brought before them and their officials to be tried and punished for minor offences. Some castles had dungeons where prisoners were kept.

A lord had the right to demand work, rents and taxes from the peasants living on his estates, but also had a duty to defend them.

Fighting was therefore very important to medieval lords. If they refused to take part in battle, they risked disgrace and dishonour.

A minstrel plays for the lord and his family

LIVING IN A CASTLE

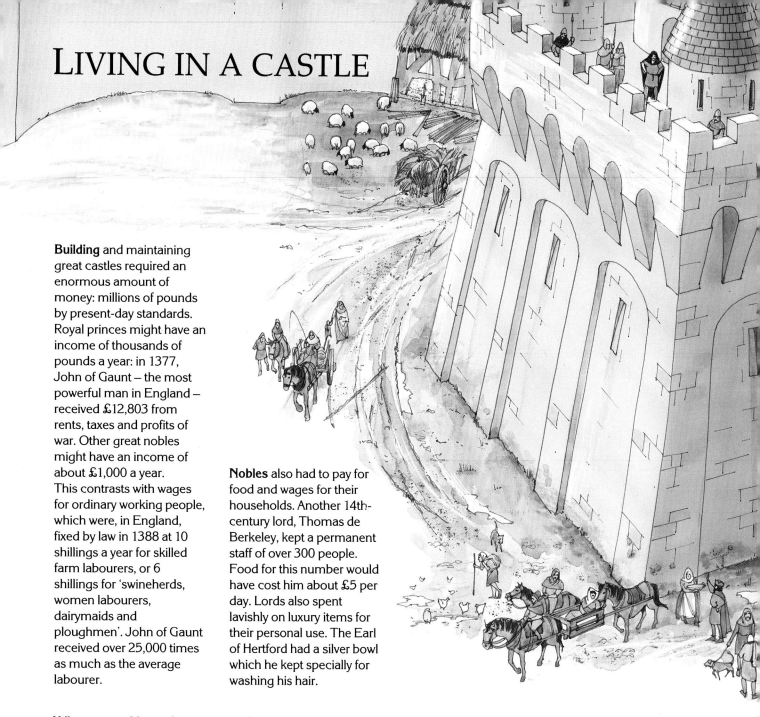

Building and maintaining great castles required an enormous amount of money: millions of pounds by present-day standards. Royal princes might have an income of thousands of pounds a year: in 1377, John of Gaunt – the most powerful man in England – received £12,803 from rents, taxes and profits of war. Other great nobles might have an income of about £1,000 a year. This contrasts with wages for ordinary working people, which were, in England, fixed by law in 1388 at 10 shillings a year for skilled farm labourers, or 6 shillings for 'swineherds, women labourers, dairymaids and ploughmen'. John of Gaunt received over 25,000 times as much as the average labourer.

Nobles also had to pay for food and wages for their households. Another 14th-century lord, Thomas de Berkeley, kept a permanent staff of over 300 people. Food for this number would have cost him about £5 per day. Lords also spent lavishly on luxury items for their personal use. The Earl of Hertford had a silver bowl which he kept specially for washing his hair.

What was it like to live in a medieval castle? Today we see them as grim ruins, open to the sky, with bitter winds whistling around their crumbling walls. But for people in the Middle Ages, a castle was the most luxurious building they were ever likely to see. As well as greater comfort and luxury, by the 14th century there was also much more privacy. The castle's inhabitants no longer ate and slept in the great hall; different members of the household had separate apartments. There were nurseries and schoolrooms for the lord's children, an elegant sitting room for the lady, a chapel, a library, and several bedrooms.

Upstairs rooms had wooden floors, plastered walls and painted ceilings – a favourite pattern was the signs of the zodiac. There might be glass in the windows, to replace the old wooden shutters. The narrow slit-windows still did not let in much light, but great lords and ladies could afford to burn tallow lamps and candles. Many rooms had fireplaces. It was cosy to sit around the glowing embers, although the most usual seats were still just hard wooden benches. Only the greatest lords and ladies had chairs. When it was time for bed, instead of a straw mattress thrown down on the cold stone floor, you would now find huge four-posters, with soft pillows filled with feathers or wool, and heavy curtains to keep out the draughts.

Solar

Library

Storerooms

Treasury

Master bedroom

Guard room

Wardrobe

Bedroom

Spinning and
weaving rooms

HUNTING AND HAWKING

'How pleasant it is, when the sun is shining brightly,
To ride out early in the morning
With keen huntsmen and hounds as my companions
Chasing the deer among the forest leaves . . .'

This was the sort of song that medieval minstrels sang to their lords. Hunting, for foxes, wolves, otters, deer or wild boar, was a passion for many noblemen. It was good exercise, but dangerous; a successful huntsman had to be brave and tireless. It provided meat for the larder and a good day's sport, if you did not mind the bloodthirsty kill.

Great nobles jealously guarded their rights to hunt in the forests, and to fish in rivers or streams. Ordinary people were not allowed to catch wild animals on their lord's estates, even if they were damaging their crops. Of course, many villagers disobeyed these rules, and went poaching.

Hunters relied on dogs' keen sense of smell to help them track down their quarry in the dense undergrowth of the forests. Dogs used for hunting were highly-bred and carefully trained. They were often very valuable. They were cared for by the lord's huntsmen and kennel-grooms, and were fed with morsels from the kill as a reward if they had helped to catch the animal.

Wild boar were found in many European forests. They could be savage when cornered, and attacked by goring men and animals with their tusks.

Equipment used when hunting wild boar:
1. Collar to protect a hunting dog's throat from the boar's tusks.
2. Spear.
3. Ivory hunting horn.
4. Huntsman's knife.

Ladies did not go hunting (except on extraordinary occasions – King John of England once bet the royal laundress that she could not follow the hunt, but she borrowed a horse and kept up with the huntsmen all day, so proving him wrong).

Ladies preferred the sport of chasing small birds with hawks. They rode out into the fields and forests, often taking a picnic of roast meat, cakes, and wine.

The poachers caught whatever they could find — hares, rabbits, squirrels and polecats. Stoats and weasels were hunted for their fur. They used ferrets and trained dogs (one convicted poacher had a dog called 'Fetch') to help them, and nets and snares to trap their prey. If poachers were caught, they were punished severely. Their right hand might be cut off, or they could be hanged.

Hawking equipment:
1. Padded glove.
2. Falconer's purse.
3. Bell to locate falcon.
4. A lure.
5. Hoods, used to calm falcon.
6. Protective linen bag for handling falcons.

RELIGION AND THE CHURCH

Religion played an important part in people's lives in the Middle Ages. Not everyone was a sincere believer, but many more people attended church then, said their prayers, and gave money to good causes in the hope of winning a place in heaven when they died. Lords and ladies spent generously on building beautiful chapels in their castles, and paid the wages of several priests. They treasured holy objects such as 'a cross of gold, wherein part of the very cross of our Saviour is contained', mentioned in the will of the Earl of Warwick (1369). Noble families helped to maintain parish churches on their estates. They paid for elaborate funeral monuments, and for prayers to be said for their souls after death. Like many people, lords and ladies went on pilgrimages, to visit the Holy Land or popular shrines. Pilgrimages were sometimes like a holiday, with pleasant inns along the route, and good company, but could be dangerous if the pilgrims were attacked by bandits, or shipwrecked.

Younger sons from noble families often made a career in the church. Bishops played an important part in government. In 1381, the Archbishop of Canterbury was also the Chancellor of England, in charge of the nation's administration. Many noble-women also held responsible positions as heads of nunneries.

1. Pilgrim, dressed in a typical long cloak and wide-brimmed hat.
2. Priests in robes worn for conducting services.
3. Bishop, wearing a mitre (a pointed hat, like a crown) and carrying a crosier (like a shepherd's crook).
4. Detail of the rich embroidery on a bishop's robes.
5. Badges worn by pilgrims.
6. Priests were expected to be well-educated. Some taught local children how to read and write.
7. Plays based on religious themes were very popular. These actors are performing the story of Adam and Eve.

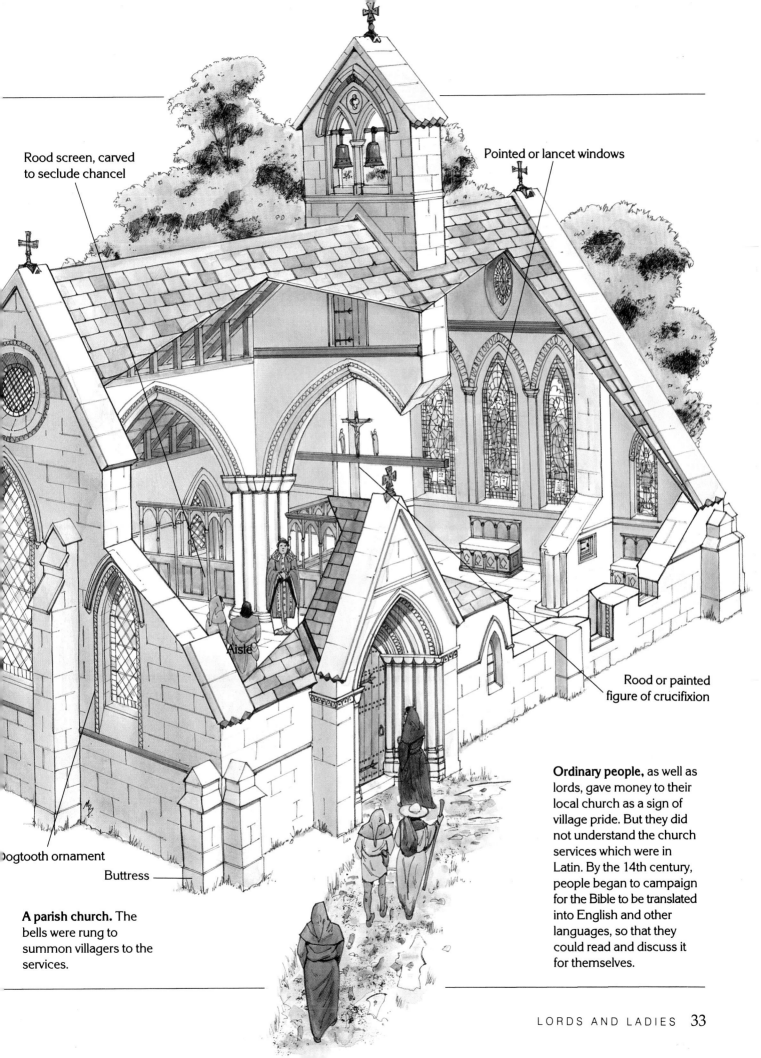

Rood screen, carved to seclude chancel

Pointed or lancet windows

Rood or painted figure of crucifixion

Aisle

Dogtooth ornament

Buttress

A parish church. The bells were rung to summon villagers to the services.

Ordinary people, as well as lords, gave money to their local church as a sign of village pride. But they did not understand the church services which were in Latin. By the 14th century, people began to campaign for the Bible to be translated into English and other languages, so that they could read and discuss it for themselves.

ARMS AND ARMOUR

In the Middle Ages, protective clothing for battle developed from chain mail (metal rings sewn on to a padded leather jerkin) to full plate-armour, made of hinged or overlapping pieces of metal.

Centre

1. Stirrups enabled a rider to swing at his opponent with a sword, without losing his seat in the saddle.
2. Arrowheads.
3. Gunther von Schwarzenberg. This mid-14th century German noble is wearing a mixture of chain and decorated plate armour.
4. Narrow-bladed dagger.
5. Heavy sword.

6. **This memorial brass** shows a French soldier of the late 14th century. He is wearing plate armour on his legs, and a padded leather jerkin under a breastplate.

Right

7. Sword belt.
8. Cap with padded roll to support metal helmet.
9. A German knight setting out on crusade (a war to capture the Holy Land from occupying Muslim forces), mid 13th century.
10. Chain mail, from the 11th century.
11. A 'coat of plates', made of overlapping metal sections, 13th century.

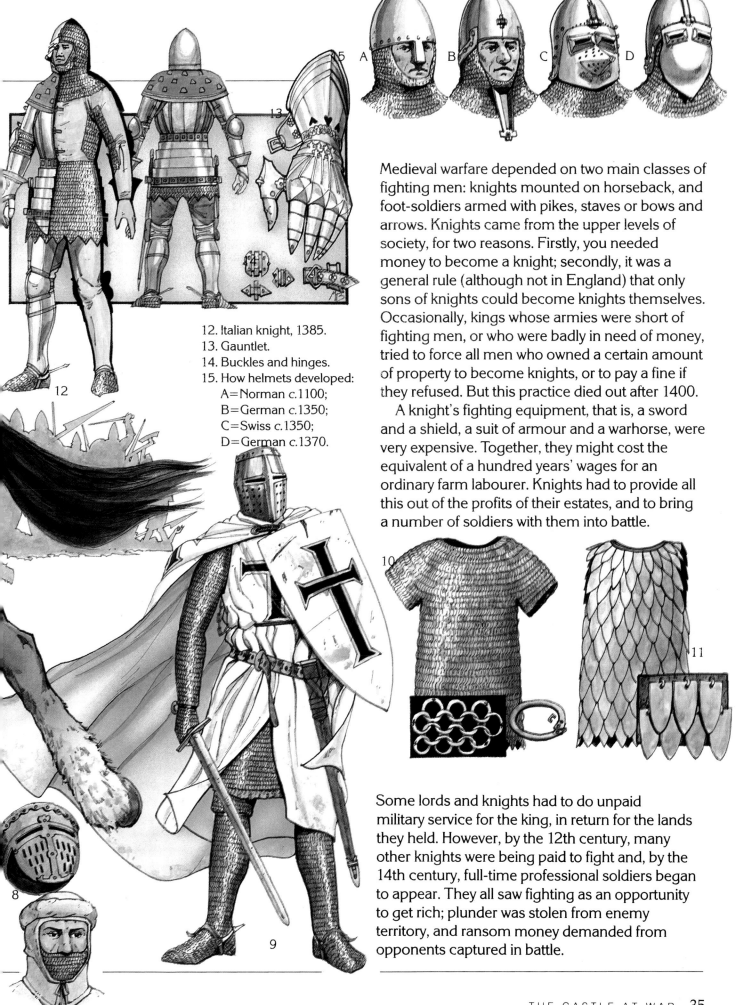

12. Italian knight, 1385.
13. Gauntlet.
14. Buckles and hinges.
15. How helmets developed:
    A=Norman *c.*1100;
    B=German *c.*1350;
    C=Swiss *c.*1350;
    D=German *c.*1370.

Medieval warfare depended on two main classes of fighting men: knights mounted on horseback, and foot-soldiers armed with pikes, staves or bows and arrows. Knights came from the upper levels of society, for two reasons. Firstly, you needed money to become a knight; secondly, it was a general rule (although not in England) that only sons of knights could become knights themselves. Occasionally, kings whose armies were short of fighting men, or who were badly in need of money, tried to force all men who owned a certain amount of property to become knights, or to pay a fine if they refused. But this practice died out after 1400.

A knight's fighting equipment, that is, a sword and a shield, a suit of armour and a warhorse, were very expensive. Together, they might cost the equivalent of a hundred years' wages for an ordinary farm labourer. Knights had to provide all this out of the profits of their estates, and to bring a number of soldiers with them into battle.

Some lords and knights had to do unpaid military service for the king, in return for the lands they held. However, by the 12th century, many other knights were being paid to fight and, by the 14th century, full-time professional soldiers began to appear. They all saw fighting as an opportunity to get rich; plunder was stolen from enemy territory, and ransom money demanded from opponents captured in battle.

TOURNAMENTS

From the 12th to the 14th centuries, tournaments, or mock battles, were a favourite entertainment for lords and their ladies. They were magnificent occasions, staged in front of a glittering audience of kings, bishops and ladies from the royal court.

Tournaments were both a way of practising for real warfare, and an elaborate, although at times deadly, game. Knights either fought in teams (called a mêlée), or in single combat (the joust). Even though combatants charged at one another with shortened lances and blunted swords, it was still quite common for them to be maimed or killed in accidents. Lords and ladies liked tournaments because they provided the chance to display everything they considered to be most important in life: membership of a noble family, skill in fighting and bravery against all odds, glamorous clothing which showed off their wealth, and obedience to a noble code of love and honour.

King Edward III of England was a great fighter, and very fond of tournaments. Accompanied by his eldest sons, he sometimes entered them in disguise. In 1343, he spent about £15 per day on living expenses, except on days when he held a tournament. Then he spent £317 on prizes, tents, horses, food and drink, and wages.

Real war was horrible, and anything but a game. Armour and padded jerkins could both be pierced by barbed arrows which tore into the flesh. Limbs could be hacked off and bellies ripped open by lances and swords. Knights were killed by falls from horses; foot-soldiers were trampled to death under their hooves. Captives were ruthlessly murdered, unless they were wealthy and could pay a good ransom.

Jousting was governed by strict rules, and there were umpires to ensure fair play. Any knight who behaved dishonourably would be disgraced.

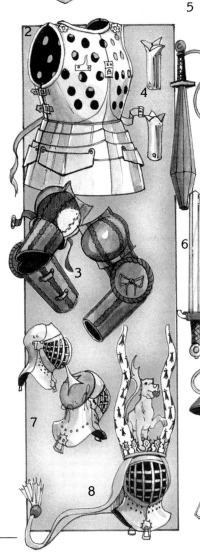

Right
Arms and armour used at a 15th-century tournament, taken from a book written by René of Anjou c.1460:

1. Heraldic crest. Originally, crests and shields (above) were badges used to identify knights wearing complete suits of armour. Later, they became highly-valued symbols of membership of the noble class.
2. Cuirass or sleeveless coat of armour, pierced with holes to lighten its weight. Battle armour weighed about 25 kilos.
3. Armguards made of specially treated leather.
4. Metal tips of tournament lances were splayed, so that they would do less damage.
5. Wooden mace.
6. Blunted sword.
7. Bassinet helmet.
8. A leather tournament cap with an iron spike fixed on top, to hold the knight's crest.

THE MAKING OF A KNIGHT

Leaving home

Toy soldiers

The skeleton of Sir Bartholomew Burghersh, who died in 1369, has been examined by archaeologists. They found that the bones of his right arm (his sword arm) were thicker and longer than his left arm. He had also suffered minor injuries in his fighting career – cracked ribs, damaged elbows and a badly twisted ankle, but no serious injuries.

It took many years' training to become a knight. A young boy from a wealthy family might be sent away to serve as a page in a noble household when he was about eight years old. He would live in the castle with other boys, under the care of a schoolmaster. They would learn good manners and social skills including singing, dancing and playing chess. They would also be taught to read and write, and some French and Latin, too.

Soon after he arrived at the castle, the young page would learn how to ride, and how to move easily when weighed down by heavy armour. He played games like tag and wrestling to build up his strength. Later, he was taught how to strike blows with a real sword, and parry them with his shield, and how to handle a heavy, pointed lance.

While they were being educated at the castle, the boys would hear tales of famous knights,

Children from wealthy families were taught to read while they were living in the castle. Reading was often a shared activity, not a private one as it is today, since medieval people usually spoke the words out loud as they read them.

Below
Knights tried to knock their enemies off their horses with a single blow from a lance. Boys practised using a lance by riding at a quintain, a shield and a straw filled sack fastened to opposite ends of a pivoted beam. If he did not hit the shield in the middle and get out of the way quickly the sack would hit him as it swung round.

Learning to read

Quintain

men who had lived and fought years ago. They dreamed of following the example of heroes like Eustace d'Aubrichecourt who, in the words of one 14th-century writer, 'performed many fine feats of arms, and often succeeded in knightly combat with noble men, nor could any one stand up to him, because he was young, deeply in love and full of enterprise [daring].' However brutal medieval warfare was in reality, this, they believed, was how the ideal knight should behave.

Below
Knights were created in different ways: a king might encourage his followers by knighting them before a battle, or sometimes afterwards, to reward men who had fought bravely. Young men who had been trained from childhood in a noble household could be created knights in a special ceremony, which included an overnight vigil, a ritual bath and an oath of loyalty to the new knight's lord and to his king.

Exercising

Knighting ceremony

Getting dressed for battle practice

FIGHTING MEN

We usually think of the typical medieval soldier as a knight on horseback, charging proudly and fearlessly towards a terrified enemy. Certainly, a cavalryman often had an advantage over a simple foot-soldier. From the safety of his horse's back, a knight could mow down single opponents. He had greater speed, weight and strength, better armour and better training than the average foot-soldier.

But massed ranks of spearmen and archers presented the knight on horseback with a more deadly foe. Even fully armoured knights and their horses were defenceless against the steady hail of arrows loosed by solid ranks of bowmen, taking shelter behind a defensive barrier. Arrows could maim or kill before knights had even started their battle charge, and so they frequently dismounted, and fought alongside the foot-soldiers. During the Hundred Years' War (c. 1340–1453), English archers won famous victories at Crécy, Poitiers and Agincourt.

Crossbows were introduced into Europe in the 11th and 12th centuries. They were so deadly that two Popes condemned them as 'unChristian weapons', and forbade their use. Crossbows fired heavy bolts which could pierce full armour at 50 metres; their only disadvantage was that they were slow to reload. For this reason, they were most frequently used in siege warfare, when bowmen could shelter behind the castle battlements while they made ready to fire again.

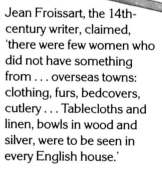

Bowman

Soldiers hoped to 'get rich quick' by looting enemy property.

Jean Froissart, the 14th-century writer, claimed, 'there were few women who did not have something from . . . overseas towns: clothing, furs, bedcovers, cutlery . . . Tablecloths and linen, bowls in wood and silver, were to be seen in every English house.'

A knight travelling with his servants

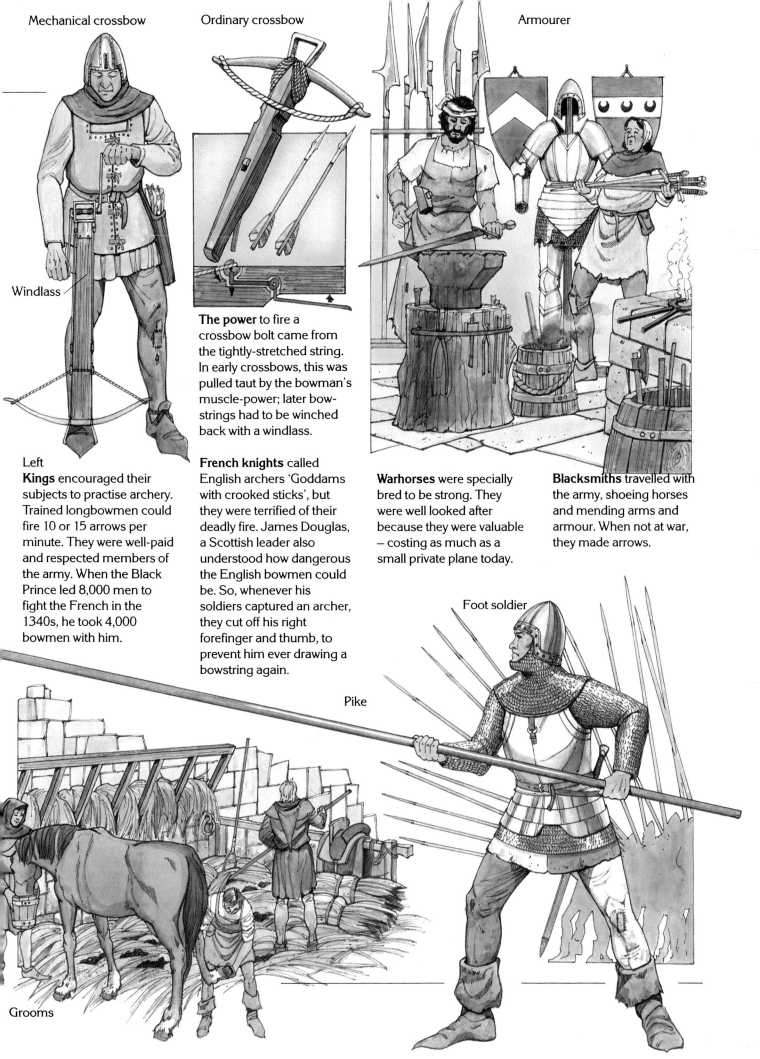

Mechanical crossbow

Windlass

Ordinary crossbow

Armourer

The power to fire a crossbow bolt came from the tightly-stretched string. In early crossbows, this was pulled taut by the bowman's muscle-power; later bow-strings had to be winched back with a windlass.

Left
Kings encouraged their subjects to practise archery. Trained longbowmen could fire 10 or 15 arrows per minute. They were well-paid and respected members of the army. When the Black Prince led 8,000 men to fight the French in the 1340s, he took 4,000 bowmen with him.

French knights called English archers 'Goddams with crooked sticks', but they were terrified of their deadly fire. James Douglas, a Scottish leader also understood how dangerous the English bowmen could be. So, whenever his soldiers captured an archer, they cut off his right forefinger and thumb, to prevent him ever drawing a bowstring again.

Warhorses were specially bred to be strong. They were well looked after because they were valuable – costing as much as a small private plane today.

Blacksmiths travelled with the army, shoeing horses and mending arms and armour. When not at war, they made arrows.

Foot soldier

Pike

Grooms

CASTLE UNDER SIEGE

Until the invention of cannon in the 14th century, castles were almost impossible to destroy. Enemy armies used a whole range of tactics to try and batter castles and to force their inhabitants into submission. They used artillery to hurl heavy stones against weak points in the castle defences, or dug tunnels underneath the castle walls, hoping to make them collapse (page 44). They scaled the outer walls using ladders and lit fires against them so that the mortar between the stones would crumble. They built siege towers, and shot arrows down into the courtyard, or through the windows.

Inside the castle, the defenders fought for their lives. They kept up a constant fire of arrows to repel their assailants – for as long as their supply lasted. They poured boiling water down onto the besiegers' heads. They launched surprise attacks to drive away the enemy soldiers. But their best hope was to stay put, and trust in the strong walls of the castle to protect them.

In fact, the besiegers' most powerful weapons were hunger, and illnesses such as typhoid or dysentery which attacked the weakened, famished defenders. The besiegers destroyed crops and livestock for miles around. They knew that sooner or later the castle would run out of food. Then the people trapped inside faced an appalling choice – death from starvation or a humiliating surrender.

A medieval castle was defended by many men. Few fortresses were as large as the famous Crusader stronghold, Krak des Chevaliers (in present-day Syria), which had room for 2,000 men.

The castle defenders lived in a state of constant uncertainty. They were cut off from contact with the outside world, and so did not know how well, or how badly, their allies were faring. The enemy forces camped outside the walls would do their best to depress them, by jeering, or by spreading false rumours. Life for the castle defenders was grim in other ways. Food was rationed, an anxious watch was kept on the well, to check that water supplies were not running low, and there was the ever-present threat of disease and malnutrition. Some sieges went on for a year or more, after which time the people inside the castle were greatly weakened by the lack of fresh food and green vegetables. In emergencies, people ate mice, rats, and even grass.

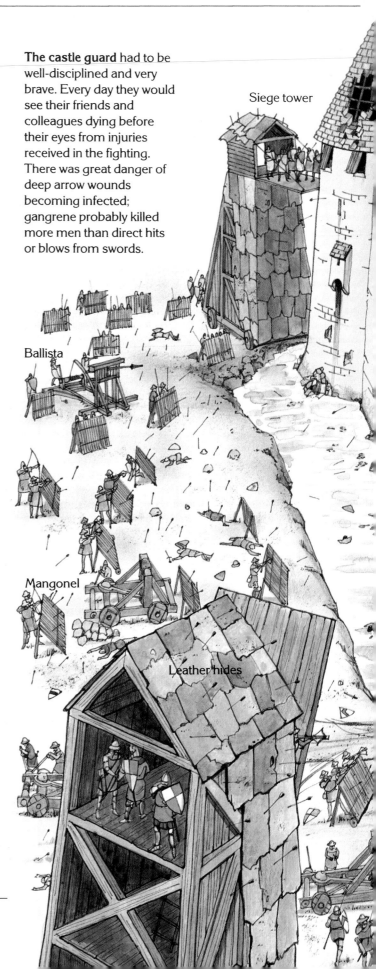

The castle guard had to be well-disciplined and very brave. Every day they would see their friends and colleagues dying before their eyes from injuries received in the fighting. There was great danger of deep arrow wounds becoming infected; gangrene probably killed more men than direct hits or blows from swords.

Siege tower

Ballista

Mangonel

Leather hides

Winch room

Drawbridge

Portcullis

Archers

Moat

Footsoldiers

THE END OF THE GREAT CASTLES

By the end of the Middle Ages, it was rare for new castles to be built. Lords and ladies might decorate their new houses with towers or battlements in the style of a castle, but only for show. Many houses designed for noble families after 1500 looked quite unlike medieval castles; they had huge windows, wide gateways, but no strong surrounding walls.

Why did castle-building stop? One reason is that castles were no longer needed as fortresses. There were still wars, but they were being fought by massed soldiers in pitched battles. In most of Europe, kings and nobles had no need of castle strongholds from which to terrorise enemy territory.

Castles were also old-fashioned. Designs for 16th-century houses were inspired by new ideas of 'civilised' living. Nobles and lords were now expected to pass their time in lively conversation about music, literature or art, discussing politics and the law, rather than fighting one another. Most important of all, castles could no longer withstand attack from the new weapons, especially cannon. Medieval castles had been costly to build, but the effort and expense was worthwhile since, once inside, the inhabitants were usually safe. But when castle walls began to crumble under cannon fire, there was no point in sheltering behind them. The age of the great castles had come to an end.

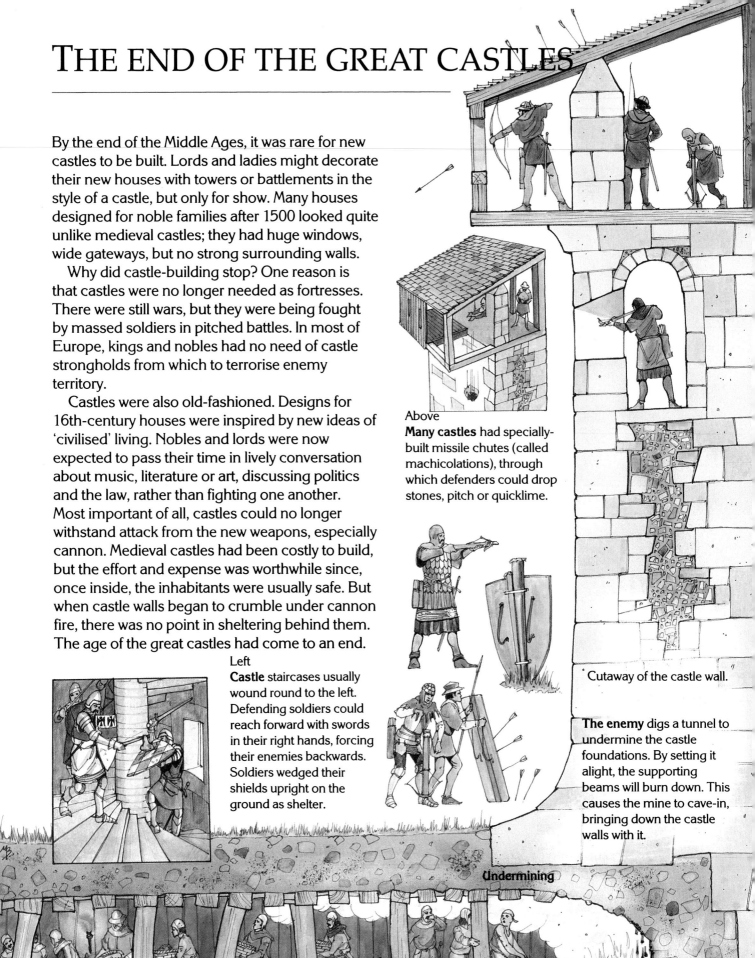

Above
Many castles had specially-built missile chutes (called machicolations), through which defenders could drop stones, pitch or quicklime.

Left
Castle staircases usually wound round to the left. Defending soldiers could reach forward with swords in their right hands, forcing their enemies backwards. Soldiers wedged their shields upright on the ground as shelter.

Cutaway of the castle wall.

The enemy digs a tunnel to undermine the castle foundations. By setting it alight, the supporting beams will burn down. This causes the mine to cave-in, bringing down the castle walls with it.

Undermining

Before leaving the tunnel, they set it on fire.

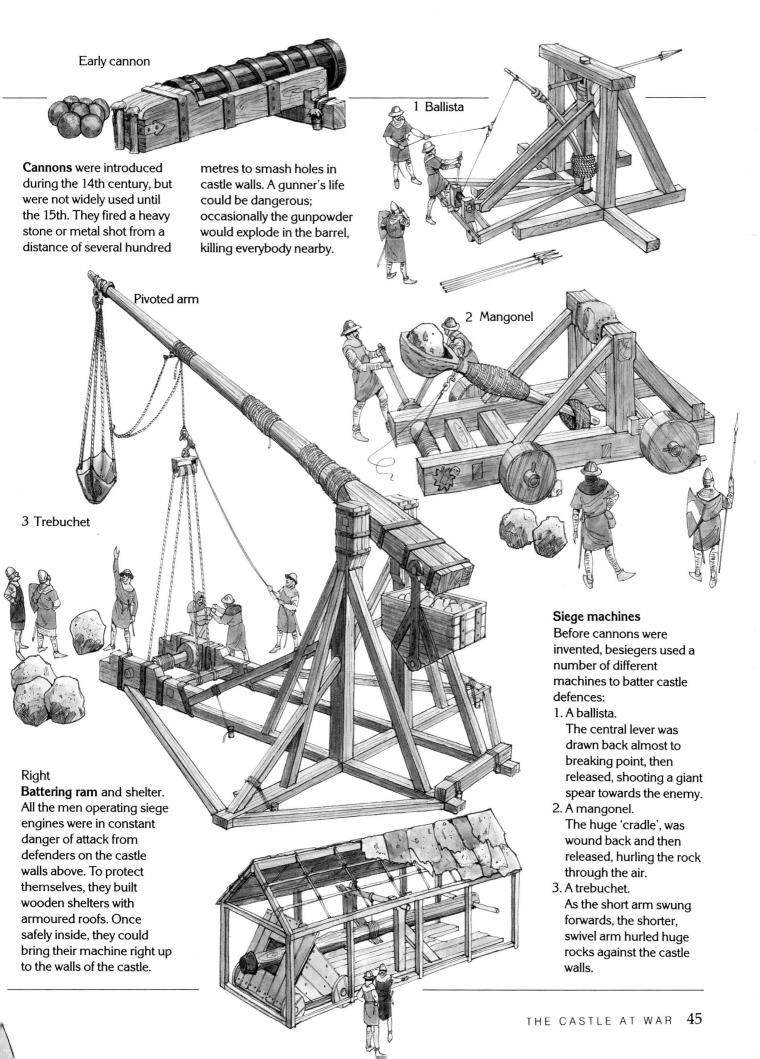

Early cannon

Cannons were introduced during the 14th century, but were not widely used until the 15th. They fired a heavy stone or metal shot from a distance of several hundred metres to smash holes in castle walls. A gunner's life could be dangerous; occasionally the gunpowder would explode in the barrel, killing everybody nearby.

1 Ballista

Pivoted arm

2 Mangonel

3 Trebuchet

Siege machines
Before cannons were invented, besiegers used a number of different machines to batter castle defences:
1. A ballista.
   The central lever was drawn back almost to breaking point, then released, shooting a giant spear towards the enemy.
2. A mangonel.
   The huge 'cradle', was wound back and then released, hurling the rock through the air.
3. A trebuchet.
   As the short arm swung forwards, the shorter, swivel arm hurled huge rocks against the castle walls.

Right
Battering ram and shelter. All the men operating siege engines were in constant danger of attack from defenders on the castle walls above. To protect themselves, they built wooden shelters with armoured roofs. Once safely inside, they could bring their machine right up to the walls of the castle.

GLOSSARY

Ashlar, cut stone blocks, used for building.

Bailey, the enclosed area surrounding a castle.

Bishop, a church leader.

Brocade, an expensive type of cloth, with a woven pattern. Brocade was often made of silk.

Chancellor, a senior government official, with particular responsibility for financial matters.

Churn, a large tub, used for making butter. It was filled with creamy milk, and shaken vigorously or stirred with an up-and-down motion, using a wooden paddle (see page 25).

Chute, slide (or hole) down which stones and boiling pitch could be hurled at an enemy.

Coffyn, the medieval word for the pastry case enclosing a pie.

Craft, the medieval word for a skilled occupation.

Daub, a mixture of clay and hair, used to cover house walls made of wattle (see page 47).

Drawbridge, a movable bridge; one end could be raised above ground, making it impossible for an enemy to cross (see page 43).

Dysentery, a disease, sometimes fatal, which caused severe sickness and diarrhoea.

Flail, a heavy, jointed stick, used to separate grains of wheat from the ears (see page 23).

Gangrene, a disease, often fatal, caused by bacteria (germs) infecting muscles and bones.

Garrison, a permanent base or lodging for troops.

Grace, a prayer said before eating.

Guild, an association of skilled workers.

Holy Land, where Jesus lived and preached. Now part of Israel, Jordan and Syria. Sacred to Christians, Muslims and Jews, for (differing) religious reasons.

Jerkin, a sleeveless jacket.

Journeyman, a skilled worker, paid by the day.

Keep, the central, or 'core', castle building.

Ling, a type of fish.

Loom, equipment used to weave cloth. It consisted of a wooden framework across which threads (the warp) were tightly stretched. The weaver wove other threads (the weft) in and out of these to create the fabric.

Lure, an artificial bird, used in training hawks for hunting.

Machicolations, another word for chute.

Masterpiece, an example of work produced by a skilled craftsman, to test whether he was worthy to be called a 'master' of his craft.

Oath, a solemn promise.

Parole, a prisoner's word of honour that he would not try to escape.

Parry, to defend yourself against a blow.

Pedlar, travelling salesperson, who carried his wares on his back. There were women pedlars, too.

Pike, a weapon consisting of a long pole topped with a curved blade and a sharp spike (see page 41).

Pilgrimage, a journey to the Holy Land or to a shrine.

Pilgrims, people who went on to pilgrimages.

Pitch, a black tarry substance; when hot, it clung to clothes and flesh and burned them.

Plunder, goods taken by soldiers from enemy territory.

Pope, head of the Roman Catholic Church.

Pullet, a young chicken.

Pungent, strong smelling.

Quicklime, a dangerous white powder that burned skin and clothing.

Ransom, a demand for money in return for a captive's freedom.

Reeds, marshland plants, used for thatching.

Ritual, a special ceremony.

Rushes, marshland plants, rather like long grass. Cut, dried and used as a floor-covering.

Scullions, junior kitchen servants who washed dirty dishes and prepared vegetables.

Scythe, a farming tool, used for cutting grass to make hay. It comprised a large curved blade fixed to a wooden handle about 2 metres in length (see page 25).

Shingle, a tile made of wood, used for roofing.

Shrine, a holy place, associated with a saint or a miracle. Often a place of pilgrimage (see page 46).

Sickle, a farming tool with a sharp, curving blade fixed to a short handle, used for cutting corn.

Shilling, in pre-decimal money, one-twentieth of a pound. A medieval shilling might be worth about £15 today. Most servants usually received free board and lodging and clothes, as well as their wages.

Stave, a long, heavy stick, used as a weapon.

Tallow, mutton fat, used for candles and lamps.

Tanned (used to describe leather), cleaned, dyed and treated to make it ready for use.

Tapestries, decorative wall-hangings, like large pictures, woven from brightly-coloured thread.

Toll, a form of tax or customs duty collected on goods for sale.

Typhoid, a disease, sometimes fatal, which caused severe sickness and a high temperature.

Undermine, to dig tunnels beneath walls or towers to make them collapse.

Venison, meat from deer.

Verjuice, sour grape juice, used like vinegar.

Vigil, a period of waiting, often including prayers; usually part of a religious service.

Wattle, woven twigs, used for house walls. It was usually covered with daub (see page 46).

Whiting, a type of fish.

Will, a legal document, giving instructions about who receives a person's property after their death.

Winch, a machine for lifting heavy weights (see illustration on page 6).

Windlass, used to tighten crossbow strings (see page 41).

INDEX

Note: page numbers in bold refer to illustrations.